DATE DUE 7·05

SEP 2 4 2005			

The Library of
ASTRONAUT BIOGRAPHIES™

JOHN GLENN

The First American in Orbit and His Return to Space

Paul Kupperberg

The Rosen Publishing Group, Inc., New York

To John Glenn and the Mercury 7.
Heroes to me then and now.

Published in 2004 by The Rosen Publishing Group, Inc.
29 East 21st Street, New York, NY 10010

First Edition

Library of Congress Cataloging-in-Publication Data

Kupperberg, Paul.
John Glenn: the first american in orbit and his return to space/Paul Kupperberg.—1st ed.
    p. cm.—(The library of astronaut biographies)
Includes bibliographical references and index.
Contents: Pioneers in flight—An American childhood—Taking to the skies—The birth of the American space program—"Godspeed, John Glenn"—The road to Washington—"A joyous adventure."
ISBN 0-8239-4460-3 (library binding)
1. Glenn, John, 1921– —Juvenile literature. 2. Astronauts—United States—Biography—Juvenile literature. 3. Legislators—United States—Biography—Juvenile literature. [1. Glenn, John, 1921–
2. Astronauts. 3. Legislators.] I. Title. II. Series.
TL789.85.G6K87 2004
629.45'0092—dc22

                                                    2003011978

Manufactured in the United States of America

CONTENTS

INTRODUCTION

PIONEERS IN FLIGHT

The United States of the 1920s was a nation celebrating its new-found position of importance on the world stage. Strengthened by a turn-of-the-century military expansion and flush with victory following World War I, America was stronger and more self-confident than it had ever been before, militarily and economically.

In that decade of unlimited, soaring potential—the exuberant Roaring Twenties—aviation became a craze, and aviators were

World War I American fighter pilot Eddie Ricken-backer prepares to take off in his Spad XIII fighter plane. Known as the "ace of aces," Rickenbacker was one of the pioneering aviators who would pave the way for the history-making triumphs of test pilots and astronauts like John Glenn.

the pop idols of the day. The mystique of aviation was fueled by tales of the exploits of such World War I aces as the United States's Captain Edward "Eddie" Rickenbacker and Germany's Manfred von Richthofen (known as the Red Baron). This enthusiasm for flight grew as air shows were held around the country and barnstormers—pilots who toured mostly rural areas in their planes—offered the locals demonstrations and rides.

Following the widespread settlement of the American West, the sky was the new frontier in need of exploration and taming. The pioneers of this frontier were aviators like Glenn Curtiss (designer and pilot of the first official public flight in the United States), Lincoln Beachey (who, in 1911, flew over Niagara Falls and broke the world altitude record in Chicago), Charles Lindbergh (who made the first solo nonstop flight across the Atlantic Ocean), Amelia Earhart (the first woman to fly across the Atlantic), and Billy Mitchell (an early supporter of the military use of airplanes).

Long before Ohio bicycle repair shop owners Orville and Wilbur Wright made the first powered flight at Kitty Hawk, North Carolina, on December

Many Americans in rural areas were first introduced to airplanes by barnstormers, who flew into small towns to perform aerial stunts and offer people rides. In this 1927 photograph, a stunt performer leaps from a car traveling at 80 miles per hour (129 km/hr) onto the wing of an airborne plane.

17, 1903, humans had been fascinated by the idea of flying. From the winged angels of biblical times to the fifteenth-century drawings of flying machines by artist and inventor Leonardo da Vinci and the nineteenth-century craze for lighter-than-air balloons, the human imagination has always been fascinated with human flight. The

Wright brothers showed the world that humans could indeed take to the skies. In the decades to come, the airplane would evolve from the first, simple 750-pound (340-kg) open-framed craft, powered by a twelve-horsepower gasoline engine, to its sleeker, far more powerful modern form we recognize today.

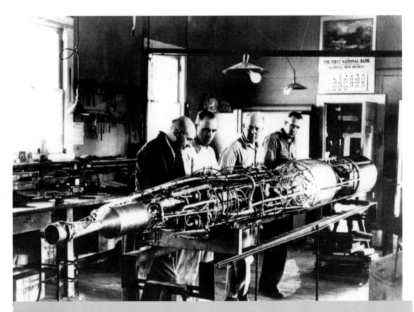

Dr. Robert H. Goddard *(far left)* and three assistants work on the fuel pump of one of his rockets. Because its casing has not yet been put on, the rocket's insides can be seen. The photograph was taken in Dr. Goddard's workshop in Roswell, New Mexico, in 1940.

While the 1920s are considered the golden age of aviation, the decade saw the birth of another mode of airborne transportation—rocketry. The world over, young men turned their sights toward the heavens, far beyond even the skies ruled by propeller-driven aircraft. Aerospace pioneers like the United States's Robert Hutchings Goddard, Russia's Konstantin Eduardovich Tsiolkovsky, and Germany's Hermann Oberth were building a foundation of knowledge that would, one day, launch human beings into outer space atop giant fire-breathing engines of unimaginable power.

Before that would happen, however, the first generation of children born after the invention of the airplane would come of age. They would grow up as wide-eyed witnesses to the development of regular air-mail routes, scheduled airline passenger service, and landmarks of aviation such as Charles Lindbergh's 1927 solo crossing of the Atlantic Ocean. They would reach maturity in a world war that saw military air power come into its own for the first time in history.

One of those children, John Glenn, born in 1921 in Ohio, birthplace of the Wright brothers,

would become the very symbol of the best and brightest that this aviation generation had to offer. As a pilot, he would be a decorated ace in two wars and a test pilot of distinction. As an astronaut, he would become the first American to orbit Earth. In later life, he would be a successful businessman before serving twenty-four years in the U.S. Senate. He would even run for president of the United States once. As a seventy-seven-year-old senior citizen, he would again undergo the exhausting strain of astronaut training and return to outer space aboard the space shuttle *Discovery*.

John Glenn's life has been characterized by dedication, courage, and service. His remarkable journey was shaped by patriotism and an idyllic upbringing in a time when human beings were speeding higher and faster through the skies than anyone had ever dared dreamed possible.

CHAPTER 1

AN AMERICAN CHILDHOOD

The first American to orbit Earth took his first airplane ride on a summer's day in 1929. The setting was an airfield outside of Cambridge, Ohio, where eight-year-old John Herschel Glenn had come with his father from their nearby home in New Concord. Glenn's father (also named John), a veteran of World War I, was there to check on a job being done by his company, Glenn Plumbing. As they drove by the grass airfield, however, they spotted something that would change the younger Glenn's life—an airplane!

To the residents of small rural American towns like Cambridge, where John Glenn had been born, and New Concord, where the family had lived

since John was two years old, the local airfield offered a rare opportunity to see a real airplane up close. Though still a novelty and not part of people's daily lives, aviation was nevertheless on everybody's mind. Just two years before Glenn's own first flight, on May 21, 1927, Charles Lindbergh had made the first solo transatlantic crossing in a specially outfitted single-seat Ryan monoplane named the *Spirit of St. Louis*. He flew nonstop from New York's Roosevelt Field to Le Bourget near Paris, France, in thirty-three and a half hours. This was an amazing journey of more than 3,600 miles (5,794 km), mostly over open ocean. When Lindbergh landed at Le Bourget at 10:21 PM Paris time, he found thousands waiting to cheer his arrival. With that single flight, Lindbergh made history and became, overnight, a celebrity the world over.

Lindbergh returned to America and received countless honors and celebrations, including a ticker-tape parade in New York City, the Congressional Medal of Honor, and, from President Calvin Coolidge, the Distinguished Flying Cross. He became a best-selling author and a popular public

Charles Lindbergh *(seated on top of backseat, without hat)* is treated to a ticker-tape parade in New York City on June 14, 1927, following his history-making solo transatlantic flight from New York to just outside Paris, France. Four million people lined the streets to welcome him home.

speaker. The modest, handsome young pilot was the most famous, sought-after man of his day.

Lindbergh's epic flight made a huge impression on eight-year-old John Glenn. Even as he imagined how scary flying might be, he couldn't help but think that it would also be a great adventure.

His first chance to find out came that summer day in 1929. The plane he and his father saw was a

WACO, a single-engine, open-cockpit biplane. Like scores of other barnstorming pilots in the 1920s, its owner traveled the country, working air circuses and making his living selling rides to people wherever he found a clear place to land.

John's father wanted to go up in the airplane. As a soldier in France during World War I, the elder Glenn had been fascinated by the planes engaged in dogfights (head-to-head midair combat) over the battlefield. Now he had the chance to experience flight for himself, with his son at his side. He was not going to let the opportunity pass him by.

After arranging the ride with the pilot, Glenn and his father strapped themselves into the backseat, and the plane soon sped down the grass landing strip. The WACO's wheels left the ground. John Glenn was flying!

The trip was short—a few circuits around tiny Cambridge from an altitude that made the town look as small as a child's toy—but it was long enough to hook the freckle-faced boy on flying forever. He resolved, one day, to take flying lessons and become a pilot.

John Glenn was born in Cambridge, Ohio, in 1921, but his family moved to this house in New Concord, Ohio, when Glenn was two years old. Today, it is the John and Annie Glenn Historic Site. *Inset:* John Glenn is nine months old in this 1922 photograph, and he already seems to be pointing toward the skies.

John Glenn's Beginnings

John Herschel Glenn Jr., was born July 18, 1921, in his parents' home in Cambridge, Ohio. He had red hair like his mother, Clara Sproat Glenn, and weighed nine pounds (4 kg). He was named after his father who, more than two years after returning

15

from the battlefields of France, became a fireman on the Baltimore and Ohio Railroad. But the elder Glenn hated being away from home so much that he quit the railroad and became an apprentice plumber. In 1923, he moved his family to New Concord and joined a local plumbing business.

John's mother was a schoolteacher who had attended Muskingum College in New Concord. Clara and John Sr. had been married on May 25, 1918, just two weeks before he had gone off to fight in World War I. They had met at the East Union Presbyterian Church near the Glenn family farm in Claysville, Ohio. Five years after John Jr.'s birth, Clara and the elder John Glenn adopted a daughter, Jean.

The younger John Glenn led what can only be described as a storybook childhood. He recalls summer days with friends, playing in open fields, climbing trees, and exploring the countryside. He remembers Sundays spent at church and in Sunday school, followed by family dinners and outings. Most of all, he remembers developing a love of country, a spirit of undying patriotism that he learned from his family and community.

Making Ends Meet

Too young to take piloting lessons, John channeled his interest in flying into building model airplanes. He even constructed a scale-model replica of the WACO he had flown in over the skies of Cambridge. All the while, he dreamed of what it would be like to climb into the cockpit and operate the controls himself. In the severe and prolonged economic depression that followed the 1929 stock market crash, however, flying lessons became an expensive luxury the Glenns could not afford. The decade-long party that was the Roaring Twenties was over. The country, so recently brimming with wealth and confidence, was suddenly shattered and impoverished.

John's family weathered the economic hard times better than many in New Concord. Thanks to federally funded loan programs, the Glenns were able to keep their house while many of their neighbors and fellow townspeople were losing theirs after failing to keep up with their mortgage payments. Mr. Glenn not only held on to the struggling Glenn Plumbing Company—even if he

BOYS TO MEN

In a town too small for a Boy Scout troop, in 1932, John and his friends formed the Ohio Rangers, a homegrown version of the Scouts. The boys met regularly, collected dues, held fund-raisers, played football and baseball against other clubs, and even built a camp in the woods. In the summer of 1933, the Rangers, after finishing their chores at home, spent most of their summer afternoons and nights at that camp, sleeping in pup tents and cooking over the campfire.

With the arrival of adolescence, John and his friends began to develop other interests, including girls. In John's case, it seemed as though there was only one girl for him—Annie Castor. Their parents had long been close friends, and Annie and John had gone from sharing a playpen to being best friends to, without even realizing it was happening, becoming a couple. By high school, Annie and John knew they were in love, a romance that began in the eighth grade and continues still, almost seventy years later.

did often work for barter rather than cash—but he also began selling new and used cars for a local Chevrolet dealership. To cut down on grocery bills, the family maintained several small gardens, including a leased two-acre plot across the road from their house, on which they grew bushels of vegetables for eating and preserving. John's family jobs included hoeing and weeding all the gardens (which he hated) and selling the family's homegrown rhubarb around town. This helped him earn some pocket money.

John also earned money washing cars. He quickly learned that, especially in hard economic times, customers expected their money's worth. The time and effort required to go back and fix a sloppy job was greater than just doing the job well the first time. After eventually saving enough money to buy a bicycle, John took on a third job—a newspaper route, delivering the *Columbus Citizen*, an afternoon daily.

The Glenns appreciated their relative good fortune in the face of the widespread suffering and deprivation of the 1930s. John's mother made sure that whatever food from the gardens not used by the family went to neighbors in need—a bag of vegetables, a pot of soup, a rhubarb pie, quietly dropped off at a neighbor's back door by John so as not to embarrass the financially troubled family.

Keeping Busy

John's love for his high school sweetheart Annie Castor still left plenty of room for other enthusiasms, especially his interest in cars. At his father's small Chevy dealership, John always volunteered to move the cars around the lot and was even given permission to help repair the used cars taken as trade-ins. The younger Glenn showed a strong talent for mechanics. At an age when he was beginning to think seriously about his future, John was unsure about what course of study to pursue in high school. He was interested and talented in mechanics, but he also felt drawn to the sciences.

Meanwhile, John also maintained a full schedule of after-school activities, including serving on the New Concord High School student council, playing on the football and basketball teams, writing for the school newspaper, and playing trumpet with the town marching band. A love for aviation remained a constant throughout Glenn's teen years, however. Along with Annie Castor, it was his other great abiding love. During family trips, he would often convince his father to stop by the Columbus airport to watch the planes take off and land. He attended the National Air Races in Cleve-

This is a senior class picture of John Glenn in 1939, the year he graduated from New Concord High School.

land and even convinced his classmates to use an aviation theme for a junior-senior banquet at his school. With family money remaining tight, however, John could still only dream about flying lessons.

In the autumn of 1939, John began his freshman year at the local Muskingum College (which his mother had also attended), majoring in engineering, with an eye toward an eventual career in medical research. Annie Castor was also enrolled in Muskingum as a music major. Between classes, an on-campus job as a maintenance worker, participation in the student council, sports, an active social

life, and dating Annie, John's life was suddenly busier than it had ever been.

A Troubled World, a New Opportunity

The world beyond the gates of Muskingum College in 1939 was increasingly frantic with activity, as well. Through the newspapers and radio, John Glenn closely followed the darkening political situation in Europe. In September 1939, Adolf Hitler's Nazi Germany invaded Poland. By the following summer, England was at war with Germany, and the skies over London were the scene of countless battles between the British and German air forces. It seemed only a matter of time before the United States would be drawn into the conflict in defense of England and France.

Though an international cataclysm, World War II provided an unexpected opportunity for John Glenn. In January 1941, in a program that was a response to the deepening war in Europe, Glenn was finally given the opportunity to fulfill his lifelong dream of flying. The Civilian Pilot Training Program

A flight instructor and his student pilot prepare for takeoff in Fort Worth, Texas, in 1942. This flight lesson was part of the Civilian Pilot Training Program, the same program that allowed John Glenn to receive pilot training in 1941.

(CPTP) was created by the U.S. Department of Commerce to train pilots who agreed, in the event of U.S. involvement in the war, to apply for military flight training. In addition to receiving free flying lessons, trainees would also receive college credits. With the help of Muskingum College physics professor Paul Martin, Glenn convinced his concerned parents to allow him to apply for the program.

Glenn was accepted into the CPTP and began his training in April 1941 at the New Philadelphia Airport in Ohio. Twenty-three-year-old Wallace Spotts was his instructor. Barely older than his college age students, Spotts introduced them to their airplane, the small, light Taylorcraft, with its sixty-five-horsepower engine capable of speeds of up to ninety miles (145 km) an hour. Step by step, two or three afternoons a week, Spotts took his trainees through the process of learning to fly, from taxiing on the runway and takeoffs to simple level flight and more complicated maneuvers. Glenn felt at home behind the joystick of the lightweight Taylorcraft, meeting every challenge his instructor threw his way. He found the complete focus required by flying to be thrilling, awakening all his senses to their fullest sensitivity.

By the beginning of May 1941, Glenn was making solo flights; by June, he had moved on to mastering difficult maneuvers and taking longer solo flights. He absorbed the Civil Pilot Training manual and achieved a grade of 96 percent on the written examination. In July 1941, he received his license. John Glenn was now a full-fledged pilot!

CHAPTER 2

TAKING TO THE SKIES

O n December 7, 1941, while driving to attend Annie Castor's organ recital at Muskingum College, John Glenn heard on the radio of the surprise attack by the Japanese air force on Pearl Harbor, the U.S. military base in Hawaii. He and Annie—and the entire nation—spent the rest of the night listening to radio reports of the thousands of sailors and soldiers killed in an aerial attack that all but destroyed America's Pacific Fleet in a matter of minutes. By the next day, in response to the "day that would live in infamy," President Franklin Delano Roosevelt proclaimed that America was now at war with Japan and Germany. When Glenn heard this, he knew what he had to do.

Airmen stationed on Ford Island in Pearl Harbor watch the USS *Shaw* burst into flames following an attack by Japanese bombers on December 7, 1941. After it was over, 2,403 American service people were dead, and 188 planes and eight battleships—most of the Pacific Fleet—were badly damaged or destroyed.

An Enlisted Man

In spite of his parent's objections and wishes that he finish college before entering the military, Glenn felt he could not wait that long. New Concord's emphasis on patriotism had greatly influenced the young man; he had come to firmly believe that military service was his duty and responsibility. As a result, Glenn went ahead and enlisted in the Army Air Corps.

Knowing he was soon to be called to active duty, Glenn did not return to college for the spring semester of his junior year. Instead, he took a job plowing fields while waiting for his orders to come through. When, by March 1942, the orders still had not arrived, Glenn enlisted a second time, this time in the U.S. Navy's air corps. Before leaving New Concord for training at the Naval Aviation Pre-Flight School at the University of Iowa, Glenn took $125 of the $130 he had made plowing and bought a diamond ring for Annie Castor. By the time he boarded the train for Iowa City, they were engaged to be married.

Naval aviation cadet John Glenn arrived in Iowa and entered the First Battalion, Company A, Platoon One, where he spent the next three months in a combination boot camp and officer training school. When not out marching and undergoing physical training, Glenn and his fellow cadets were in classrooms, studying such subjects as navigation, aero-dynamics, and engineering. American involvement in the war was now in full swing, with fighting raging along fronts in Europe, Asia, and the Middle East. All branches of the military were in a rush to get men through training as quickly as possible so they could be sent to the various hot spots.

After three months in Iowa, Glenn was sent to Olathe, Kansas, for flight training in a Stearman, a larger, more powerful plane than the little Taylor-craft in which he had learned to fly. He was trained to fly at night, in formation with other planes, and under all sorts of harsh flying conditions. Classroom studies continued as well, and three months later, Glenn was off to the Naval Air Training Center in Corpus Christi, Texas, for basic and advanced flight training.

In Corpus Christi, Glenn began to think about transferring from the navy to the marines. The celebrated marine tradition of strength and pride appealed to the young aviator. After graduating from cadet training in the top 10 percent of his class in both air and ground instructions, he felt ready to join this elite branch of the service. Glenn, along with his friend and fellow cadet, Tom Miller, applied and was accepted. At the end of March 1943, Glenn received his wings and his commission as a second lieutenant in the marines. Several days later, on April 6, during a fifteen-day leave back home in New Concord, John Glenn and Annie Castor were married.

From "Flying Boxcars" to Fighter Jets

The newlyweds reported to Glenn's new duty station at the Marine Corps Air Station in Cherry Point, North Carolina. Once there, he began training to fly the North American B-25 Mitchell, a twin-engine medium-range bomber that carried five to seven crew members, five gun turrets, and 3,000 pounds (1,361 kg) of bombs.

From Cherry Point, Lt. Glenn was next sent to the Naval Auxiliary Air Station at Kearney Mesa, California, where he was assigned to a transport squadron flying R4D cargo planes. Cargo planes were the huge, slow-moving workhorses that ferried soldiers, equipment, and supplies to the war's front lines. Piloting large "flying boxcars" was not what John had joined the marines to do, however. He was a natural flier, a pilot who felt that a plane's

controls were an extension of his own body. Despite the vitally important role cargo planes played in waging WWII, the giant, lumbering R4D was not Glenn's idea of a precision aircraft.

Glenn's transport group shared an airfield with VMO-155, a fighter squadron that flew Grumman F4F Wildcats, planes that had played a decisive role in the Battle of Midway. The Wildcats called to Glenn from across the field, and he went after, and attained, a position in the VMO-155 squad. While the R4D plodded along through the skies, responding sluggishly to its controls, the F4F was a speedster, sensitively reacting to the slightest touch of the joystick at some 350 miles (563 km) per hour.

This fighter training would serve John Glenn well when, on February 5, 1944, he kissed his new wife good-bye and boarded the USS *Santa Monica* to set sail with the rest of VMO-155 for the Pacific and his first taste of combat.

Glenn's Pacific War

Lieutenant John Glenn arrived at Majuro, the Marshall Islands, in the North Pacific in July

In April 1943, John Glenn married his high school sweetheart and longtime family friend Anna Margaret Castor. Together they would have two children, John David (in 1945) and Carolyn Ann (in 1947), and two grandchildren. They remain married to this day.

1944. Majuro was one of a series of atolls (a coral island that encircles a lagoon) that had seen some of the fiercest fighting during the early days of the war with Japan. By the time the marines of VMO-155 arrived, the Americans had captured the largest and most strategic of these atolls, but isolated Japanese forces still held several of the smaller islands.

Glenn flew the first of his fifty-nine combat missions within days of his arrival on Majuro, staging a raid on Japanese antiaircraft guns on nearby Maloelap. The marines would fly one or two missions a day, attacking Japanese positions or outfitting their powerful Corsairs to serve as dive-bombers, dumping 1,000-pound (455-kg) bombs on the enemy. Glenn excelled at combat flying and found bombing runs to be "a test of skill, nerve, preparation, and focus" that he relished, as he said in *John Glenn: A Memoir.* In November 1944, VMO-155 moved to Kwajalein in the continuing campaign to attack enemy positions and forces in the Marshall Islands.

During his tour of duty in the Pacific, Glenn earned two Distinguished Flying Crosses. In early 1945, he was rotated back to the United States (pilots flew only a fixed number of missions before being sent home) and assigned to Patuxent River Naval Air Station (known as Pax River), the newly commissioned testing facility in Cedar Point, Maryland. There, Glenn learned the skills necessary to become a test pilot.

DANGER AND DARING

Test pilots were very prestigious and dashing figures in the late 1940s and 1950s. They were the heirs to the mystique of aviation pioneers like Lindbergh and Earhart. In order to test the newest experimental fighter jets that the armed forces began developing during and after World War II, they took enormous risks in unproven machines at great speeds and dizzying altitudes. It took a special brand of pilot to be admitted into this select club of mavericks. A successful test pilot had to have the grit necessary to suit up and fly in a super-powerful but untested machine that had never been off the ground before. As a result, test piloting soon became one of the glamour careers of the postwar years, and one of the most dangerous.

A Return to War

The U.S. military was only beginning to fly newly developed jet aircraft in the last months of the war. Soon after his arrival at Pax River, Glenn found himself behind the sticks of such experimental planes as the F8F Bearcat and the Ryan Fireball FR-1. He could not have been happier with this turn of events. At Pax River, Glenn also received a promotion to captain and decided to try to make a career for himself in the Marine Corps.

After a two-year stint in Guam, Glenn found himself back in the United States, stuck at a desk job. Five years after the end of World War II, the real action was now occurring in Korea, where, in June 1950, Communist North Korea invaded the democratic southern portion of the divided nation. The United Nations voted to send troops in support of South Korea, with the majority of the military might supplied by the United States.

Impatient to get back in a cockpit, Glenn began pestering his superiors with requests for transfer to a fighter squadron in Korea. His persistence paid off, and in February 1953, he joined the First

This is a portrait of John Glenn in uniform as a lieutenant in the U.S. Marine Corps. Glenn flew fifty-nine missions during World War II. After serving two years as a flight instructor, he volunteered for the Korean War. He flew sixty-three missions and shot down three North Korean MiGs.

Marine Air Wing, VMF-311, piloting the F9F Panther, in P'ohang, Korea. The F9F, capable of speeds up to 604 miles (972 km) per hour, was a powerhouse compared to the propeller-driven F4U Corsair he had flown over the Marshall Islands. Armed with 3,000 pounds (1,361 kg) of bombs and five-inch (12.7-cm) high-velocity missiles, the F9F

was perfect for ground attack missions. Stationed only 180 miles (290 km) from the war's front lines, the Panthers flew frequently in support of marine troops on the ground. Glenn counted among his fellow pilots in VMF-311 the legendary Boston Red Sox slugger Ted Williams, whose professional baseball career was interrupted by both World War II and the Korean War.

Glenn had several close calls on these support missions, limping back to base on more than one occasion with flak or shell holes punched through his aircraft. Despite these brushes with danger, Glenn still wanted to see more action. He liked the discipline and challenge of flying ground support, but he yearned for a chance to engage in air-to-air combat.

The "MiG Mad Marine"

Captain Glenn was finally put to the test when, after flying sixty-three missions with VMF-311, he applied for a special exchange program to fly F-86 Sabre interceptor jets with the air force. Assigned to the 25th Fighter Interceptor Squadron at Suwon,

This is a photograph of John Glenn's F-86F Sabre. The three stars painted just below the cockpit's windscreen represent the three MiG-15s he had shot down in Korea. The names Lyn, Annie, and Dave are also painted on the plane's side in tribute to his daughter, wife, and son.

Glenn helped patrol "MiG Alley," an area south of the Yalu River in northwestern Korea. The air corridor earned this nickname because it was the route the Soviet–built North Korean MiG–15 fighters flew from their bases in Manchuria, just over the border with China. MiG Alley was the scene of hundreds of encounters between Sabres and MiGs. Glenn had little initial luck in encountering any of the opponent's aircraft, however. His complaints about the absence of MiGs led his air force colleagues to dub him the "MiG Mad Marine," even painting the nickname on the nose of his Sabre.

By the middle of 1953, Glenn was leading two- and four-plane sorties (flight missions). On July 12, he spotted and chased a MiG-15 over the Yalu River into Manchuria, shooting it down as it attempted to land. The MiG Mad Marine had his first air-to-air "kill"—the downing of an enemy fighter (often, enemy pilots were able to eject and parachute to safety). Several days later, Glenn and seven other F-86s were surprised by a squad of sixteen MiGs, leading to a full-fledged aerial dogfight. Glenn soon scored his second kill, followed on July 22 by the downing of a third MiG. In Korea, this already decorated World War II pilot would earn his third Distinguished Flying Cross and eight Air Medals for his service.

Just five days after Glenn's third MiG kill, on July 27, 1953, an armistice (a cease-fire) was declared by the United States and North Korea after two years of difficult negotiations. The Korean conflict was ended, though no actual permanent peace treaty was ever signed. At war's end, Glenn returned home and threw himself right back into the world of test piloting. He attended Test Pilot School at the Naval Air Test Center, Patuxent River, Maryland. Upon completion of his courses, Glenn was promoted to major and spent more than two years assigned to the Fighter Design Branch of the Navy Bureau of Aeronautics in Washington, D.C. On top of all this work and study, Glenn was trying to be a good husband to Annie and father to their children, John David (born in 1945) and Carolyn Ann (1947).

The Cold War and the Race for Space

The year 1957 was to be a major turning point in the life of John Glenn and in the larger history of the world. In the years following the end of World War II, a new war broke out, but this was a very different sort of conflict. It became known as the Cold War—a long period of simmering tension and distrust between the United States and

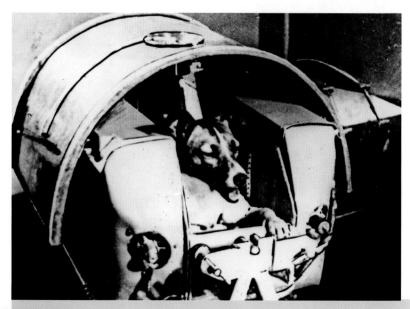

A dog named Laika (Russian for "barker") was launched aboard *Sputnik II* on November 3, 1957, by the Soviet Union. She was the first living creature from Earth to travel into space. Sadly, the Soviets had not created any way to return Laika to Earth, so she died in space about a week after the launch.

the Soviet Union (today Russia and several other former Soviet republics). Each nation tried to export its political ideas to the other nations of the world. The United States tried to foster and protect democracy, while the Soviets pushed Communism. Though the two superpowers never actually fired a single shot at each other (hence, it was a "cold" war), they often supported and fought with other nation's armies in conflicts—such as the Korean and Vietnam Wars—that in part represented the struggle between democracy and Communism. The Cold War required the super-powers to build and maintain a large and high-tech arsenal of weapons for use in case war broke out between them. This arms race was soon matched by a growing space race.

On October 4, 1957, the Soviet Union shocked the world with the launch of *Sputnik*, the first artificial satellite to be sent into orbit around Earth. The tiny satellite, less than two feet (0.6 m) across, did nothing more than orbit the planet once every ninety-six minutes, transmitting a steady beeping tone by radio signal. Though limited in usefulness, the 184-pound (83-kg) metal ball raised great worries in the United States and Europe about a future that might include Soviet space stations controlling the world. The United States soon responded with satellites of its own. Even more ambitious and breathtaking was the nation's new resolve to launch a series of programs that would feature manned spaceflights and the landing of men on the Moon! John Glenn hoped to take part in

OR J.H. GLENN, USMC
PROJECT BULLET

John Glenn poses in the cockpit of his F-8 Crusader. Soon after this jet entered service, John Glenn piloted it in an experimental, nonstop flight from Los Angeles to New York City. With the help of three midair refuelings, he would set a coast-to-coast speed record.

this new space program. His passion for flying and piloting experimental aircraft would soon carry him farther and higher than any fighter jet ever could.

CHAPTER 3

THE BIRTH OF THE AMERICAN SPACE PROGRAM

During the early months of 1958, the National Advisory Committee on Aeronautics (NACA) put out word that its research center at Langley Air Force Base in Virginia was looking for test pilots with extensive flight experience to help flesh out the outlines of a new manned space program being developed. These pilots would basically serve as guinea pigs, undergoing tests and training that would try to determine how the human body would perform when placed under the stressful conditions of space travel. They would also help engineers and designers create a spacecraft that could send a man into space and return him to Earth safely. This early in the process, no one was even certain what

shape such a program would ultimately take. NACA was actively testing the X-15, a winged rocket plane, while the air force was pushing its Man In Space Soonest (MISS) program—a multi-phase, manned space program that resembled what would eventually become the Mercury, Gemini, and Apollo projects.

Becoming a Space Pilot

John Glenn, still attached to the Fighter Design Branch in Washington, D.C., requested the NACA assignment and found himself suddenly thrust into another world. He began to learn the rules of orbital mechanics—how to achieve orbit, and once there, how to control a ship in the zero gravity of space. Most important, he would master the techniques necessary for a safe reentry and landing of the spacecraft. Reentry from the zero-gravity conditions of space into Earth's dense atmosphere is a violent, difficult, and extremely dangerous process.

Glenn's few days at Langley led to a trip to the Naval Air Development Center in Johnsville, Pennsylvania. There he climbed into a pod attached to the end of the fifty-foot (15-m) arm of a centrifuge. A centrifuge is a machine that spins an object around in circles at a very high rate of speed. The resulting pressure placed upon the object is known as centrifugal force. As Glenn was strapped into the pod and whipped around by the centrifuge, his body was subjected to centrifugal forces that simulated the force of gravity (called G forces) that he would experience during liftoff and reentry of a space

This is a centrifuge-mounted simulator of the sort that John Glenn was strapped into to test his reaction to the physical stresses of space travel. The centrifuge's arm would spin the simulated capsule attached to its end at increasing speeds until the astronaut trainee reached the limits of his endurance.

capsule. Pilots also experience the crushing weight of these G forces during acceleration, especially in supersonic jets. Even civilians experience G forces every day. G forces are what press us back into the seats of our cars during rapid acceleration. Many of the latest roller coasters and thrill rides subject their riders to several Gs. As a pilot, Glenn had routinely experienced four to six Gs (four to six times the force of gravity ordinarily felt on Earth) and sometimes as much as eight or nine (the amount one experienced in a space launch).

Having proven that the human body can withstand a heavy load of G forces for at least a brief period of time, Glenn was next temporarily attached to the McDonnell Aircraft plant in St. Louis, Missouri, where he worked on the design of the proposed space capsule. It had been decided that the fastest way to get a man into space was by the ballistic approach—to use rockets to hurl a manned capsule beyond the force of Earth's gravity. At McDonnell Aircraft, Glenn represented the interests of the pilots who would be flying that capsule. There was some concern about just how much actual piloting these men would be able to perform. Some

In the late 1950s, the U.S. Air Force gathered a colony of captured wild chimpanzees at the Holloman Air Force Base in New Mexico. These chimpanzees were to be used to test the effects of space travel on humans. Three-year-old Ham, seen above, was the first chimp to travel to space on January 31, 1961.

scientists were doubtful whether a man would be able to function, physically or psychologically, in orbit. They felt onboard computers needed to be able to perform all the guidance functions in case the astronaut got sick or confused.

Glenn felt confident that a pilot could function as well in zero gravity as he could on Earth. He had no interest in being sent up into space without having any piloting job to perform other than sit and enjoy the view. He did not want to be part of a publicity stunt. If the nation was serious about developing a manned spaceflight program, he wanted the spacecraft pilots to fly their craft. As a result, he did everything he could to ensure that the capsule's manual controls met his high standards.

On loan as a test pilot from the marines to the newly formed NASA in 1959, John Glenn helped design and test an early version of the Mercury capsule before he had even applied to be an astronaut. After serving as adviser on this project, Glenn decided to apply to NASA's astronaut program.

Despite the fact that the research and development for the manned spaceflight program was well underway and men like Glenn had become deeply involved in its progress, President Dwight D. Eisenhower had yet to formally commit himself. "If there had been a call for volunteers, I would have been at the front of the line," Glenn said in *John Glenn: A Memoir*. Instead, he found himself frustrated, participating in a fascinating program with an uncertain future. And, he had to admit, he was finding his own future rather uncertain as well: "I was almost thirty-seven years old, a United States Marine Corps major stuck in a desk job," as quoted in Glenn's memoir.

Finally, after several long, uncertain months, one source of Glenn's anxiety was removed. On July 29, 1958, President Eisenhower signed into law the National Aeronautics and Space Act. At long last, the United States was firmly committed to sending men into space.

Making the Grade at NASA

The National Aeronautics and Space Administration (NASA) was established in October 1958 as a governmental agency committed to manned spaceflight and exploration. The agency hit the ground running with a $100 million budget, numerous facilities, and 8,000 employees. While rockets and spacecraft were being designed and the agency planned its series of manned space-flight programs, the search began for NASA's first group of space pilots.

As NASA worked its way through the records of 508 military test pilots, John Glenn remained in the running. At a top secret Pentagon briefing, he and the other candidates were told what lay ahead for the program's volunteers. These men, to be called astronauts (literally "star voyagers"), would be the guinea pigs in the first manned suborbital and orbital space flights. A suborbital flight would send a capsule high into Earth's atmosphere. An orbital flight would place the capsule higher than Earth's atmosphere into the zero gravity of space where it would then begin to circle above Earth. Scientists could only guess what space travel might do to the human body. They did not yet know how they were even going to launch these men into space, how they were going to bring them back, and if they would survive the journey. NASA engineers needed to gather together and train a select group of the country's best, brightest, and bravest pilots to help find the answers to these crucial questions.

John Glenn—and dozens of pilots like him— accepted the dangers and uncertainty and volunteered for the new space program. The man who had always felt the lure of the open sky now had a new challenge to master, a new envelope to push, a new frontier to explore.

Glenn survived round after round of elimination in the astronaut corps and finally was told to report for medical tests at the Lovelace Clinic in Albuquerque, New Mexico. He was instructed to travel in civilian clothes and was given a number to use instead of his name when checking in upon arrival. The clinic put the candidates through the most demanding medical and physical examinations imaginable. "They drew blood, took urine and stool samples, scraped our throats, measured the contents of our stomachs . . . and submerged us in water tanks to record our total body volumes," Glenn reported in his memoir. "They shone lights into our eyes,

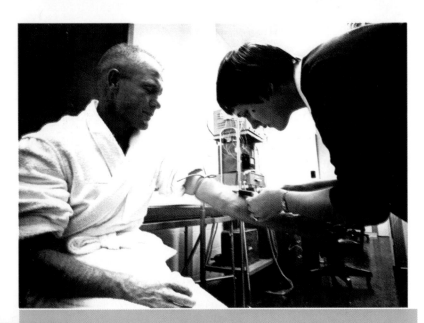

NASA nurse Delores B. O'Hara takes blood from John Glenn at Cape Canaveral, Florida, during the long training process leading up to his Mercury spaceflight. Most of the Mercury 7 astronauts grew weary of NASA's physical prodding and psychological tests.

ears, noses, and everywhere else. They measured our heart and pulse rates, blood pressure, brain waves, and muscular reactions to electric current . . . Nobody wanted to tell us what some of the stranger tests were for."

Though all this poking, prodding, and probing was uncomfortable, Glenn survived his eight days at Lovelace and moved on to Ohio's Wright–Patterson

Air Force Base and the Development Center's Aeromedical Laboratories for a series of stress tests. These involved everything from being placed in heat tanks to spending long stretches in isolation chambers. Everything was designed to test the trainees' reactions to the extreme conditions—both known and supposed—of space travel. Psychological testing was also performed to find candidates with the cool, calm, and collected attitude necessary for the risky and stressful job.

On April 6, 1959—John and Annie's sixteenth wedding anniversary—Glenn received the phone call for which he had been waiting. United States Marine Corps major John Glenn had been selected to train as an astronaut for the NASA space program.

CHAPTER 4

"GODSPEED, JOHN GLENN"

I n the spring of 1959, seven men were chosen by NASA to participate in the space agency's first manned spaceflight program—Project Mercury. The Mercury 7—as the first generation of American astronauts came to be known—met for the first time at Langley Air Force Base on April 8, 1959. Joining John Glenn were Lieutenant Commander Alan B. Shepard (U.S. Navy), Lieutenant M. Scott Carpenter (U.S. Navy), Lieutenant Commander Walter "Wally" Schirra (U.S. Navy), Captain Leroy G. "Gordo" Cooper (U.S. Air Force), Captain Virgil I. "Gus" Grissom (U.S. Air Force), and Captain Donald K.

"Deke" Slayton (U.S. Air Force). All seven expected their new assignment to be the most challenging of their already impressive careers. What they had not expected was the fame and attention that came with being a Mercury astronaut.

The Mercury 7

On April 9, NASA presented the Mercury astronauts to the world at a press conference in Washington, D.C. The usually cynical and unimpressed Washington press corps gave them a standing ovation, and that was only the beginning of the startlingly enthusiastic public reaction. Newspapers across the country and around the world trumpeted the selection of these seven brave men, and journalists raced to learn all they could about them.

Amid the distractions of all this media and public attention, the astronauts were trying to remain focused and work extremely hard to prepare their bodies, minds, and spacecraft for manned space flight. Fellow Mercury 7 astronaut Scott Carpenter trained alongside Glenn and served as backup on his Mercury flight. In his memoir *For Spacious Skies*, Carpenter recalled Glenn's determination: "Glenn

John Glenn was in the Mercury program with six other former test pilots. These six Mercury astronauts pose here before a model of the Mercury capsule. From left are Gordon Cooper, Wally Schirra, Gus Grissom, Deke Slayton, Scott Carpenter, and Alan Shepard.

was a machine, like no one [I] had ever competed against, roomed or argued with, flown or run miles with." Glenn attacked every problem—from his boyhood car-washing business in New Concord to training to ride a rocket into outer space—in the same manner, with laser-sharp focus, intense concentration, and boundless energy.

Hands-on Involvement

Bob Gilruth, head of the Space Task Force, had promised the astronauts direct day-to-day involvement in the development of the space program and their spacecraft. He proved true to his word. In addition to astronaut training, studying, maintaining a schedule of flying, and individual physical fitness programs, each astronaut was assigned a specialized area of responsibility for the mission. Because of his experiences with a wide variety of jet aircraft, Glenn was put in charge of cockpit layout and instrumentation, spacecraft controls, and simulations.

There was not a single part of the rocket or capsule, or a single phase of the mission that did not reflect the input of at least one of the seven astronauts. As part of this hands-on development process, they visited the contractors building the spacecraft and consulted on design and mechanics with engineers and workers on the assembly lines. These seven men were trusting their lives to new, untested technologies, and they wanted to be certain that no system was overlooked, no possible problem was unplanned for, no defect went undetected.

Mercury training continued throughout 1959 and 1960, ranging from mock missions in simulators to survival training in the ocean and desert. "We all spent hours on our backs in the trainers as we ran through launch simulations again and again," Glenn remembered in his memoir. "We trained system by system, until we were capable of running them all together on simulated missions."

Once the astronauts had mastered the spacecraft's systems, the training staff began to throw emergency situations their way. "They seemed to take fiendish pleasure in thinking up new emergencies for us to react to—oxygen failures, launch aborts, electrical system failures, control system failures, early aborts, and emergency reentry," Glenn said in his memoir.

Falling Behind

Glenn was fairly confident that he would be chosen for the first manned suborbital flight. He felt he had worked and studied hard and proven himself worthy of earning an assignment to the

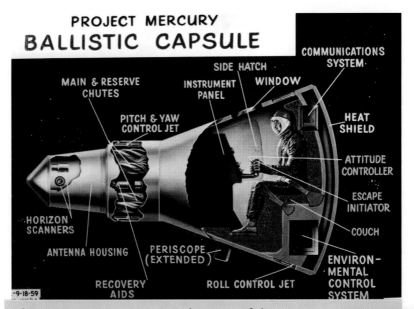

PROJECT MERCURY
BALLISTIC CAPSULE

COMMUNICATIONS SYSTEM

SIDE HATCH

MAIN & RESERVE CHUTES

INSTRUMENT PANEL

WINDOW

PITCH & YAW CONTROL JET

HEAT SHIELD

ATTITUDE CONTROLLER

ESCAPE INITIATOR

HORIZON SCANNERS

COUCH

ANTENNA HOUSING

PERISCOPE (EXTENDED)

ENVIRON-MENTAL CONTROL SYSTEM

-9-18-59

RECOVERY AIDS

ROLL CONTROL JET

This is an artist's cut-away drawing of the Mercury capsule. Some of the most important features and manual controls—such as the parachutes, communications system, instrument panel, heat shield, and steering controls—are clearly labeled. Most important, the illustration gives a good sense of just how cramped the Mercury capsule was.

very first American manned space flight. To his great disappointment, however, Alan Shepard won the desired spot on the first manned Mercury mission. Glenn and Gus Grissom were scheduled to follow him into space, in an order yet to be determined. In order to keep attention focused on the spaceflight, rather than on any particular astronaut, the choice of Shepard for the number

MAKING HISTORY AND
MOVING FORWARD

On May 2, 1961, NASA publicly announced that Alan Shepard had been selected for the first Mercury mission. On May 5, a Redstone rocket fired perfectly and hurled the astronaut and his *Freedom 7* capsule almost 116 miles (187 km) into space. Only fifteen minutes later, Shepard splashed down in the Atlantic Ocean as planned. NASA had proved that it could launch a human into space and return him to Earth, safe and unharmed.

Following this successful mission, President John F. Kennedy took the opportunity to go before a special joint session of Congress on May 25 and declare, "I believe that this nation should commit itself to achieving the goal, before this decade is out, of landing a man on the Moon and returning him safely to the Earth."

Kennedy had suddenly raised the stakes with these words. Catching up to the Soviets and matching their orbital flights was no longer enough. The United States wanted to beat the Soviet Union in space and pull off an almost unimaginable feat—the first manned Moon shot in history.

one spot was kept a secret from the public until just before the flight.

Then, on April 12, 1961, an event took place that made personal considerations about which American went first into space seem far less important. Soviet cosmonaut (the Russian term for "astronaut") Senior Lieutenant Yuri Gagarin became the first human being in history to leave Earth's atmosphere behind and enter outer space aboard the *Vostok 1* spacecraft. He spent 108 minutes in a single orbit around Earth at an altitude of some 187 miles (301 km). The Soviet Union had once again beat the United States in a crucial leg of the space race. Even worse, not only was the first man in space a Russian, he was a Russian who had orbited the planet! NASA was not planning an orbital flight until several missions into the Mercury program. The Soviets seemed to have pulled far ahead of the American space program.

The United States would have to scramble to catch up with its Soviet rivals. "They just beat the pants off us, that's all, and there's no use kidding ourselves about that. But now that the space age has begun, there's going to be plenty of work

Alan Shepard poses in his Mercury pressure suit before becoming the first American to enter space during the *Mercury-Redstone 3* spaceflight on May 5, 1961.

for everybody," Glenn wrote in his memoir. Rather than jeopardize astronaut lives, NASA resisted the temptation to alter the Mercury program and achieve orbital flight sooner than planned. Instead, it stuck to the methodical, step-by-step mission progression it had originally planned. The first suborbital flights would test the rocket and capsule technology and establish that NASA could send an astronaut into space and return him safely. Having proven itself in a series of suborbital missions, NASA would then proceed carefully to its more ambitious orbital flights.

The First American in Orbit

The space race was on. John Glenn was itching to participate in his portion of the race, but he found himself having to wait. Gus Grissom had been selected to pilot Mercury's second manned mission. Grissom's *Liberty Bell* 7 capsule followed Shepard's *Freedom* 7 on an almost identical mission and was—except for some post-splashdown difficulties—as successful as its predecessor. NASA had established that Shepard's spaceflight was no fluke. Its astronauts and its space program undeniably had the "right stuff."

After a second manned Soviet orbital mission on August 6, 1961 (in which Major Gherman Titov flew seventeen orbits in twenty-five hours), NASA decided it was time to move on to the next phase of manned spaceflight. Though assigned to third position, John Glenn would soon be piloting a history-making spaceflight, perhaps the most important mission of the entire Mercury program.

On February 20, 1962, after ten countdown delays caused by weather and technical difficulties, John Glenn's *Friendship* 7 capsule (a name chosen by his children) lifted off from Cape Canaveral atop its Atlas booster rocket at 9:27 AM. As the rocket left the pad, Scott Carpenter spoke the words that conveyed the anxious, hopeful wishes of people the

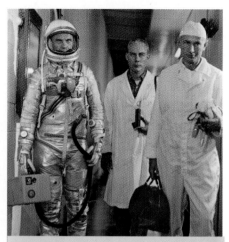

John Glenn, in his pressure suit and helmet, leaves crew quarters with the flight surgeon *(center)* and an equipment specialist on his way to the launch pad and his *Friendship 7* capsule.

world over: "Godspeed, John Glenn."

"I had thought the booster might lift off so gently that there might be some doubt as to when you were actually moving; but there's no doubt about it, you know when you come off the pad," Glenn later wrote in his postflight report to NASA. "When the Atlas releases, there's an immediate surge—gentle surge—that lets you know you're underway."

John Glenn, aboard *MA-6 (Mercury Atlas-6)*, was indeed underway on a historic flight. He was about to become the first American to orbit Earth. The flight would last four hours, fifty-five minutes, and twenty-three seconds, and reach an altitude of some 162 miles (261 km), at an orbital velocity of approximately 17,500 miles (28,163.5 km) per hour, for a total distance of

Friendship 7, with John Glenn aboard, takes off from Cape Canaveral, Florida, on February 20, 1962. During the *Mercury-Atlas 6* mission, Glenn would become the first American to orbit Earth. At age 40, he was the oldest of the seven Mercury astronauts, but his experiences with space travel were far from over.

75,679 miles (121,794 km). The orbital flight, the first of its kind for NASA, would prove to be anything but routine.

Problems Arise

Just before completing his first orbit, Glenn reported a problem with the capsule's automatic guidance system. "[T]he capsule started drifting . . . then the high thruster would kick on and bat it back over to the left. It would overshoot to the left and then it would hunt and settle down again somewhere around zero. The spacecraft would then drift again to the right and do the same thing repeatedly," Glenn wrote in his post-flight report to NASA. Glenn's capsule had a faulty attitude control system. This guidance system was supposed to automatically fire thrusters that kept the spacecraft at its proper attitude (position relative to Earth) and course.

Glenn was forced to take manual control of the capsule before the malfunction burned too much fuel and jeopardized the mission. Fortunately, he found that the hundreds of hours he had devoted to training on the NASA simulators had prepared him well for the job. He would operate the controls for most of the rest of the mission, including the difficult and dangerous process of reentry into Earth's atmosphere.

A White-knuckle Landing

In the third hour of the spaceflight, mission control sent Glenn a mysterious message: "Keep your

An onboard camera snapped this picture of John Glenn in the *Friendship 7* capsule during the *Mercury-Atlas 6* space flight. He is using a photometer—an instrument that measures the intensity of light—to view the sunset outside his capsule window. He had also packed a camera and binoculars to help him make observations from the spacecraft.

JOHN GLENN

landing bag position in off position." The landing bag contained the heat shield on the blunt bottom of the capsule. This shield protected the spacecraft from the extreme heat generated during reentry. Over the shield were fastened retro-rockets that were fired to slow down *Friendship 7* before reentry. As the capsule slowed, it would fall out of orbit and begin to descend, passing through the dense and superheated atmosphere of Earth on its way to splashdown. Glenn, busy flying his craft and performing experiments and observations, thought little of this request. A short time later, he was asked to again confirm that his landing bag switch was off and whether he had heard any banging noises. He checked the switch and said that he had not heard any noises but had no idea why he was being asked these questions.

He found out soon enough. As *Friendship 7* was preparing for reentry, mission control informed him, "We have been reading an indication on the ground of segment fifty-one, which is landing bag deploy." If the indicator light was correct, it meant, according to Glenn, as quoted in his memoir, "that the heat shield that would protect the capsule from

68

the searing heat of reentry was unlatched . . . The package of retro-rockets that would slow the capsule for reentry was strapped over the heat shield. But it would jettison (after firing), and what then? If the heat shield dropped out of place, I could be incinerated on reentry." But for all his suspicions about what the problem might be, no one on the ground was telling the craft's pilot what was happening or just how serious the situation was.

Mission control waited until moments before reentry to inform Glenn of their suspicions of a loose heat shield. The capsule began to get uncomfortably hot. This might have been a normal rise in temperature during reentry, but in light of a possible heat shield problem, Glenn began considering the worst-case scenario. To add to the tension, he would be on "fly-by-wire," or full manual control for the rest of the ride down to Earth. He could not rely on computers and an automatic guidance system to steer the tricky way back home.

As designed, the straps holding the retro-rockets in place gave way, melting quickly in the intense heat. A thump was all the evidence Glenn had

John Glenn and *Friendship 7* splashed down in the Atlantic Ocean after an almost five-hour space-flight. At left, the capsule is pulled from the water by a helicopter. At right, Glenn is lowered to the deck of the USS *Randolph* from a marine helicopter after being pulled from the water.

that the pack had jettisoned. Without the help of these straps, only the air pressure beneath the plummeting craft could hold the heat shield in place, if in fact it had come loose. As the capsule plunged back through the thickening atmosphere, the air around it turned red hot, blacking out communications between Glenn and mission control. "Through the window, I saw the glow [around the capsule] intensify to a bright orange. Overhead, the sky was black. The fiery glow wrapped around the capsule," Glenn wrote of the descent in his memoir.

At twelve miles (19.3 km) altitude, air resistance slowed the capsule to subsonic speed (slower than the speed of sound). At about 28,000 feet (8.5 km), the drogue parachute opened, further slowing him down. At 10,000 feet (3 km), the large main chute opened, and *Friendship* 7 floated down at forty feet (12 m) per second toward the planned Atlantic Ocean landing site, only six miles (9.7 km) from the recovery ship, USS *Noa*. The heat shield warning had been a false alarm.

A Hero's Welcome

John Glenn rode *Friendship* 7 into orbit as a member of an elite class of pilots. Less than five hours later, however, he splashed down in the Atlantic as an international hero on the scale of his boyhood idol, Charles Lindbergh. Unlike secretive Soviet spaceflights that were only announced after the fact, the entire world had watched Glenn take his extraterrestrial journey. He became a very visible and charming symbol of NASA's program and ideals.

Vice President Lyndon B. Johnson was sent to escort Glenn home from Grand Turk Island, where he had been taken after being picked up by the USS *Noa*. The astronaut was greeted everywhere he went with cheers and celebrations. He addressed both the United Nations and a special joint session of Congress (an honor usually reserved for royalty or heads of state) and was treated to a ticker-tape parade in New York City along Broadway—the "Canyon of Heroes." Finally, President Kennedy awarded Glenn with NASA's Distinguished Service Medal.

The nation was in love with John Glenn, and many opportunities presented themselves as a result. Robert "Bobby" F. Kennedy, the president's brother and U.S. attorney general, tried to convince Glenn to run for one of Ohio's U.S. Senate seats. But Glenn decided to stick with NASA. He had just gained rare flight experience that would be useful to the remaining Mercury flights, and he was part of the team planning the cockpit design of the Apollo capsule. Project Mercury proved that man could fly and function in space. Now the upcoming Project Gemini (with two-man crews) would develop hardware and procedures for the eventual

ASTRONAUT
JOHN GLENN

John Glenn's Personal Album

LIFE
MAKING OF A BRAVE MAN

Due to both his hard work and skill with the press, John Glenn became one of the most popular Mercury 7 astronauts, both before and after his historic orbital spaceflight. At top, he appears on the cover of *Life* magazine less than three weeks before the launch of *Mercury-Atlas 6*. At bottom, he is treated to a ticker-tape parade in New York City soon after his safe return to Earth.

President John F. Kennedy *(far right)* and Vice President Lyndon B. Johnson *(second from right)*, along with Democratic Congressional leaders, watch a live broadcast of the launch of John Glenn and *Friendship 7*. Because of Glenn's national popularity, Kennedy tried to persuade Glenn to launch a political career.

Apollo (three-man) missions that would put a man on the Moon.

Glenn also stayed at NASA because he hoped to earn a place on another spaceflight. Even with the addition of nine new astronauts to the space program, he felt sure that he would be offered a second flight. The answer he received time and time again to his requests, however, was "not yet."

The reason for this, which he was only to learn years later, was that President Kennedy had decided that the first American in orbit was too much of a "national asset" to risk on future missions. If John Glenn became the victim of a space disaster, the American space program would be dealt a terrible emotional and psychological blow. It was felt that Glenn could do more for manned spaceflight on Earth than up among the stars. His charisma, personality, and fame would be used to create and maintain public interest in the nation's long, difficult journey to the Moon.

In effect, John Glenn, the world's most famous pilot and astronaut, had been grounded.

CHAPTER 5

THE ROAD TO WASHINGTON

Throughout the summer of 1963, Bobby Kennedy had spoken to John Glenn about the possibility of the astronaut running for public office. The attorney general and his brother, President Kennedy, felt that Glenn stood a good chance of winning the 1964 Democratic primary for a Senate seat from Ohio. A Glenn candidacy would strengthen the Democratic Party in Ohio, not to mention increase the president's support in the state in the 1964 presidential election.

Glenn remained committed to the space program, however. Then, on November 23, 1963, the unimaginable happened—President Kennedy was assassinated in Dallas, Texas. Glenn, in shock and mourning, took a long, hard look at his own life. He and Annie finally concluded that it was more important than ever for good people to enter public life. As Scott Carpenter remembered in his memoir, "Personal ambition about a lunar mission suddenly seemed selfish. John and Annie soon resolved that he would run for the U.S. Senate; a seat was opening up in 1964. Three months later he resigned from NASA, and soon the Glenns were throwing themselves into the Ohio Democratic primary. They had a good shot at winning."

A Race Cut Short

On January 17, 1964, John Glenn threw his hat into the political ring, announcing that he was seeking the Democratic nomination for senator in Ohio. The current senator, Stephen Young, was seen as very vulnerable, especially against someone Scott Carpenter described in his memoir as "the most popular and recognized man on the planet." Little more than a month into the campaign, however,

Glenn slipped on a bathroom rug and hit his head on the shower door's metal track running along the bathtub ledge. He suffered a concussion that caused swelling and bleeding in the inner ear, affecting his balance. "Any but the slowest of head movements would make the whole world spin," Glenn recalled in his memoir. "I was virtually immobile."

It would take Glenn many months to recover, and he did not feel up to running a campaign from his sickbed. He withdrew from the race on March 30, 1964, deciding that it made more sense to heal first and run again in the next election. Senator Young went on to win the election by a mere 16,000 votes over his Republican challenger. Glenn was left with no plans for the immediate future and a campaign debt of $16,000 (money the candidate would repay from his own pocket). Meanwhile, he still had a family to support. His oldest son, Dave, was about to enter Harvard University, where tuition and living expenses would be high.

For a man as famous and beloved as John Glenn, however, it was only a matter of time before opportunity came knocking. Though he

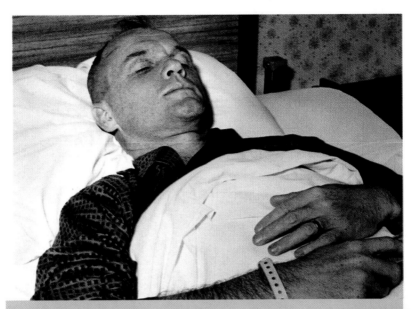

The first political campaign of the first American to orbit Earth was cut short by an accident—a slip and fall by the tub. Glenn is seen here recovering from the severe concussion that forced him to withdraw from the 1964 Ohio Senate race. Like his astronaut career, however, his political career was far from over.

had received many tempting offers to endorse products ranging from automobiles to sporting goods to breakfast cereal, Glenn did not wish to profit from his fame. Nor would he have been content "to be simply a pitchman for some product or some company. I wanted a job in which I could actually learn something about business, where my opinion counted for something and I could be involved in making decisions," as he said in his memoir. He found exactly what he was looking for with Royal Crown Cola, where he served as a member of its board of directors and vice president for corporate development.

Fully recovered by October, Glenn received a promotion to full colonel in the Marine Corps from President Lyndon B. Johnson at a White House ceremony. He then officially retired from the corps on January 1, 1965, after twenty years of distinguished service. During this time, Glenn continued to make public appearances in support of NASA and the space program. His job at Royal Crown and his work with the Boy Scouts of America and other public service organizations kept Glenn busy and often on the road.

John Glenn Goes to Washington

Another national tragedy struck close to home for the Glenns in June 1968 when their friend Bobby Kennedy was assassinated in a hotel kitchen while campaigning in California for the Democratic presidential nomination. John and Annie were

DEATHS IN THE NASA FAMILY

On February 1, 1967, John Glenn's Mercury 7 comrade, Gus Grissom (*center*), along with astronauts Ed White (*left*) and Roger Chaffee (*right*), died in the fire that consumed the *Apollo 1* spacecraft during a preflight test. "The space program had gotten off Earth and was reaching for the Moon," Glenn said of those sad days in his memoir. "Tragically, our friends were gone." The American space program had experienced its first loss of life. The race to the Moon went on, however, to be won by the United States with *Apollo 11*. Neil Armstrong and Buzz Aldrin's historic lunar landing in July 1969 fulfilled President Kennedy's challenge to Americans to put a man on the Moon by the end of the 1960s.

traveling with Kennedy at the time and watched the events unfold on television in a suite several floors above the kitchen. They would also be on hand the next day to deliver the news to the Kennedy children that their father had died. Glenn would serve as one of the pallbearers at Kennedy's funeral.

John Glenn *(right)* and close friend Robert F. Kennedy take a break during a kayaking trip down the River of No Return in Idaho in 1966. The assassination of John F. Kennedy convinced Glenn to get into politics. Less than two years after this picture was taken, Robert would be assassinated, too, and Glenn would break the terrible news to Kennedy's young children.

Glenn's resolve to lead a life of public service was further strengthened by Bobby Kennedy's death. In 1974, he was elected by the state of Ohio to the U.S. Senate by a two-to-one margin over his Republican opponent. Glenn would win reelection in 1980 (with the largest majority in Ohio history) and 1986. In 1992, he became the first popularly elected senator from Ohio to win four consecutive terms. Always looking for the next frontier to conquer, Senator Glenn began setting his political sights even higher. In 1980, he was a contender for the vice presidency in the Carter campaign, and in 1983, he announced a run for the presidency. Despite an early strong showing in the polls against fellow Democrat and former vice president Walter Mondale, Glenn's campaign never really picked up momentum. On March 16, 1984, after poor showings in the early primaries, he dropped out of the race.

Though far less dramatic and pulse-pounding, Senator Glenn's Senate service was as successful as his military and NASA careers. Glenn jumped into the work of shaping policies regarding nuclear technology, energy management, and the Strategic

Arms Limitation Treaty (SALT; an arms–reduction agreement between the United States and the Soviet Union). He was one of the prime movers behind the Nuclear Non–Proliferation Act (limiting the worldwide spread of nuclear weapons) and introduced legislation that created the Defense Nuclear Facility Safety Board to improve health and environmental safety standards in the nuclear industry. He served, at various times, on the Foreign Relations Committee, the Committee on Energy and the Environment, the Governmental Affairs Committee, the Select Committee on Intelligence, the Armed Services Committee, and the Special Committee on Aging. Because of his engineering and astronaut background, he was considered the Senate's resident expert on technical and scientific matters.

This record of achievement in government was marred by a single hint of scandal, when, in 1987, Glenn was investigated for alleged ethics violations relating to the then collapsing savings and loan industry. He was suspected of receiving improper campaign contributions from a banker involved in the scandal. The investigation dragged

After serving for nine years as one of Ohio's senators, John Glenn decided to run for president in the 1984 presidential race. He is seen here during a campaign parade in Mason City, Iowa, in July 1983. His campaign did not go very far, and Glenn returned to the Senate. This turned out to be a lucky break. Toward the end of his political career, his work in the Senate suddenly revealed to him a way he could plot a return to space.

on for three years before he was finally and fully cleared of any wrongdoing. Glenn continued to serve in the Senate with great distinction for another ten years. One day, nearing the end of his Senate career, he stumbled upon information that would help carry him out of the Senate chamber and back into space.

Planning a Return to Space

In 1995, Senator Glenn was reviewing materials for an upcoming International Space Station (ISS) funding debate. The ISS is a large laboratory that orbits Earth and is a temporary home and office to visiting astronaut-scientists who conduct research in space. Sixteen nations, including the United States, Russia, Japan, Canada, and Brazil, and the European Space Agency came together to fund, build, and staff the ISS. Construction of the ISS began in 1998 and has continued through 2003.

In the course of preparing for the debate, Glenn read *Space Physiology and Medicine*, a book written by three NASA doctors, which listed and described fifty-two different types of physical changes that happen to astronauts in zero gravity. The list included balance disorders, osteoporosis (bone-mass loss), disturbed sleep patterns, cardiovascular changes, and many others. It occurred to the seventy-three-year-old legislator and veteran of the Special Committee on Aging that these ailments were similar to the effects of aging on the elderly. He began to wonder if the study of zero-gravity-related ailments could result in breakthroughs for elderly health care and if preventive measures offered to astronauts in orbit could have similar positive effects for the elderly on Earth. Most important, he began to wonder how zero gravity would affect the health of an elderly person.

Believing these questions deserved further investigation, Glenn spoke with the NASA doctors who wrote the book, as well as a variety of experts in geriatric medicine (health care for the elderly). It seemed to the senator that there was room for exploration in this area. Once again, he hoped he would be the one to cross the frontier.

In the course of regular budget meetings with NASA director Dan Goldin, Glenn began pitching his proposed space study on the similarity of the effects of zero gravity and aging on the human body. He also took the opportunity to present his reasons for believing that he should be the one to fly this particular mission. He even pressed his agenda with President Bill Clinton during a 1996 presidential campaign stop in Ohio. The president would have to approve any mission Glenn might take.

On February 20, 1997, Glenn marked the thirty-fifth anniversary of his historic Mercury spaceflight to announce his intention to retire from the Senate at the end of his current term. He was seventy-six years old and had led an amazing life. He had proven successful in not one, or even two, but four different careers over the course of his lifetime, from pilot to astronaut to businessman to politician.

Retirement did not mean John Glenn was finally ready to settle down. He decided he still had one more job to do—return to space!

"A JOYOUS ADVENTURE"

John Glenn knew from the start that he would have an uphill battle convincing NASA to give him—a seventy-seven-year-old man—a seat on the shuttle. First, he needed to prove that he was physically up to the challenge. Second, he had to establish that the mission he was proposing was scientifically valid and worthwhile. He demonstrated his remarkable physical fitness by putting himself through as thorough a physical examination as he had ever undergone in his life, including checks of his heart, liver, kidneys, pancreas, and brain.

With these reassuring exam results, Glenn met again with NASA director Goldin and pitched his scientific program. Goldin agreed to review Glenn's proposal and meanwhile sent him to the Johnson Space Center to undergo the same demanding and exhausting physical tests that any astronaut would be required to take before being cleared for flight. As Glenn knew they would, the NASA doctors gave him a clean bill of health. With momentum for his cause gaining, NASA's scientific review board approved Glenn's experimental agenda. A news conference on January 16, 1998, made it official: John Glenn was going back into space!

A New Crew, a New Mission

He was assigned to the crew of the space shuttle *Discovery* as a payload specialist on mission STS-95, a nine-day flight scheduled to launch on October 29, 1998. The announcement set off a storm of excitement within the press corps that reminded Glenn of his early days as one of the Mercury 7. One of the first men in outer space and America's first man in orbit, Glenn was now almost twice the age

This is a portrait of the crew of STS-95, the shuttle mission that would return John Glenn to space. Seated from left are mission commander Curtis Brown and pilot Steven Lindsey. Standing from left are mission specialists Scott Parazynski and Stephen Robinson, payload specialist Chiaki Mukai, mission specialist Pedro Duque, and payload specialist John Glenn.

he had been when he first left Earth's atmosphere. Once again, he was thrust into the spotlight. Though he could not deny being thrilled at finally being allowed to return to space, he was also genuinely excited about the scientific experiments he would be conducting while in orbit.

The experiments would focus on several areas in which the aging process and spaceflight experience share a number of similar physiological responses, including bone and muscle loss, balance disorders, sleep disturbances, and weakened immune systems. Glenn hoped that by observing how zero gravity causes these ailments in astronauts, scientists would gain a better understanding of the basic processes of aging. The changes in the body that occur in space reverse themselves following an astronaut's return to Earth. Discovering how these reversals occur might also help scientists discover how to reverse the same conditions in the earthbound elderly.

Glenn joined a team of shuttle astronauts as elite as the original Mercury 7. He would fly with mission commander Lieutenant Colonel Curtis L. Brown Jr. (U.S. Air Force), pilot Lieutenant Colonel Steven W. Lindsey (U.S. Air Force), mission specialist Dr. Stephen K. Robinson (Ph.D.), flight engineer and mission specialist Dr. Scott E. Parazynski (MD), mission specialist and European Space Agency (ESA) astronaut Pedro Duque, and payload specialist Dr. Chiaki Mukai (MD, Ph.D.) from the Japanese Space Agency (NASDA).

On October 29, 1998, John Glenn returned to space onboard the space shuttle *Discovery* during the mission STS-95. Once the oldest of the Mercury 7 astronauts, John Glenn was now the oldest human ever to journey into space. Once again, John Glenn was soaring far beyond Earth and making history among the stars.

Glenn was able to hold his own against his far younger crewmates. He found the physical exercise demanding but fun. He was well prepared for the rigors of training. In the many years that had passed since his first acceptance into NASA, he had never stopped his daily exercise program (though running had been replaced by power walking in recent years), including training with the free weights that

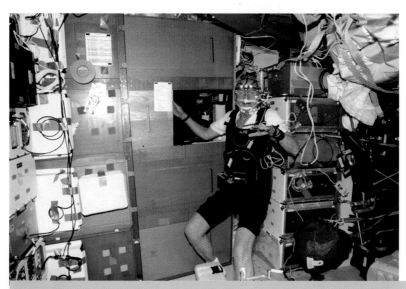

John Glenn's shuttle flight was not a publicity stunt. He was sent into space to perform a series of scientific studies on the aging process. Glenn is seen here hooked up to sleep monitoring equipment. In order to help identify the factors contributing to sleep problems in astronauts and the elderly, Glenn's sleep patterns were monitored before, during, and after spaceflight.

he had first picked up during his Mercury training days. Once again, he climbed aboard the centrifuge, although at half the G forces he had experienced in his Mercury days. The space shuttle provided a far gentler liftoff and reentry than had his old Atlas rocket.

On October 29, 1998, payload specialist John Glenn rode the space shuttle *Discovery*, with its 7 million pounds (3.2 million kg) of thrust, back into outer space. This journey would last almost nine days, taking the veteran astronaut some 3.68 million miles (5.9 million km) in 134 Earth orbits and producing results in his orbital aging experiments that are still being studied.

A Lifetime of Accomplishment

In his long, rich, and busy life, John Glenn has flown farther, higher, and faster than even he had ever dreamed possible. His contributions to piloting, space exploration, and government have been recognized the world over, nowhere more so than at home, where the New Concord High School was renamed in his honor. Muskingum College

now features the John Glenn Gymnasium, and Highway 83, on which his boyhood home was located, is now called Friendship Boulevard (after his *Friendship* 7 capsule). The stretch of Interstate 40 in Ohio between his birthplace in Cambridge and his home in New Concord has been designated John H. Glenn Memorial Highway.

Even his successful return to space at the age of seventy-seven did not signal Glenn's retirement. Instead, he continues to promote space exploration and participates in a number of public and charitable causes. Among many other honors and appoint-ments, Glenn is an honorary member of the International Academy of Astronautics, an inductee to the Aviation Hall of Fame and National Space Hall of Fame, a member of the Society of Experimental Test Pilots, a member of the Ohio Democratic Executive Committee and the Tenth District (Ohio) Democratic Action Club, an elder of the Presbyterian Church, and a trustee of Muskingum College.

In addition to pioneering space travel, John Glenn has achieved what few Americans ever have—he has bridged the generation gap. Because

John Glenn appears at a press conference at the Kennedy Space Center in Florida one day after his return from space onboard the space shuttle *Discovery*. Behind him is a poster of Glenn in his Mercury spacesuit from almost forty years earlier. Upon his return, Glenn's wife, Annie, said she hoped this marked the end of his flying days.

of his two widely separated historic trips to outer space, he is a familiar and beloved face to almost all living Americans. For people of all ages, the name John Glenn conjures the smiling image of a heroic figure clad in a high-tech space suit, eager to take the next thrilling step into the unknown. And, to John Glenn, the distance traveled from his first brief flight in an open cockpit, single-engine plane in 1929 to his nine-day voyage aboard a spacecraft that featured the very latest in aerospace technology almost seventy years later must truly seem like the greatest leap of all.

GLOSSARY

Atlas booster   A ballistic missile modified to carry spacecraft payloads instead of warheads.

barnstormer   A 1920s and 1930s aviator who flew from place to place, offering plane rides and exhibitions to the public.

Civilian Pilot Training Program   Prior to World War II, a program of the U.S. Department of Commerce to train civilian pilots who agreed to enlist in the armed forces as military pilots in the event of war.

Distinguished Flying Cross   A medal awarded to officers and warrant officers for an act or acts of valor, courage, or devotion to duty performed while flying in active operations against the enemy.

drogue parachute   A small parachute used to stabilize a space capsule's descent, slowing the capsule before the main parachute deploys.

flak   Antiaircraft fire from ground-based guns.

fly-by-wire   Taking manual control of a space-craft; operating the hand-controller to change the position of the space capsule.

heat shield   A protective layer attached to the blunt end of a spacecraft that protects the capsule from the heat of reentry; made of a material that will melt as it carries the heat away from the spacecraft.

retro-rockets   Small rocket thrusters used to slow a spacecraft down, allowing it to fall out of orbit and begin reentry into Earth's atmosphere.

subsonic   Slower than the speed of sound.

supersonic   Faster than the speed of sound.

FOR MORE
INFORMATION

American Astronautical Society
6352 Rolling Mill Place, Suite 102
Springfield, VA 22152-2354
(703) 866-0020
Web site: http://www.astronautical.org

Goddard Space Flight Center
Code 130, Office of Public Affairs
Greenbelt, MD 20771
(301) 286-8955
Web site: http://www.gsfc.nasa.gov

Jet Propulsion Laboratory
4800 Oak Grove Drive
Pasadena, CA 91109
(818) 354-4321
Web site: http://www.jpl.nasa.gov

The John and Annie Glenn Museum and
    Exploration Center
P.O. Box 107
New Concord, OH 43762
(740) 826-3305
Web site: http://muskingum.edu/~jglenn/

The John Glenn Institute at Ohio State University
1947 College Road
Columbus, OH 43210
(614) 292-4545
Web site: http://www.glenninstitute.org

Johnson Space Center
Visitors Center
1601 NASA Road 1
Houston, TX 77058
(281) 244-2100
Web site: http://www.jsc.nasa.gov

Kennedy Space Center Visitor Complex
Mail Code: DNPS
Kennedy Space Center, FL 32899
(321) 449-4444
Web site: http://www.kennedyspacecenter.com/
    index.html

NASA Headquarters
Information Center
Washington, DC 20546-0001
(202) 358-0000
Web site: http://www.nasa.gov

National Air and Space Museum
Seventh Street and Independence Avenue SW
Washington, DC 20560
(202) 357-2700
Web site: http://www.nasm.si.edu

National Association of Rocketry
P.O. Box 177
Altoona, WI 54720
(800) 262-4872
Web site: http://www.nar.org

Space Policy Institute
1957 E Street NW, Suite 403
Washington, DC 20052
(202) 994-7292
Web site: http://www.gwu.edu/~spi

U.S. Space Camp
P.O. Box 070015
Huntsville, AL 35807-7015
(800) 533-7281
(256) 721-7150
Web site: http://www.spacecamp.com

United States Strategic Command
Public Affairs
250 S. Peterson Boulevard, Suite 116
Peterson Air Force Base, CO 80914-3190
(719) 554-6889
Web site: http://www.spacecom.mil

Web Sites

Due to the changing nature of Internet links, the
Rosen Publishing Group, Inc., has developed an
online list of Web sites related to the subject of this
book. This site is updated regularly. Please use this
link to access the list:

http://www.rosenlinks.com/lasb/jgle

FOR FURTHER READING

Bond, Peter. *DK Guide to Space.* New York: Dorling Kindersley Publishing, 1999.

Bredeson, Carmen. *John Glenn Returns to Orbit: Life on the Space Shuttle.* Berkeley Heights, NJ: Enslow Publishers, Inc., 2000.

Bredeson, Carmen. *John Glenn: Space Pioneer.* Brookfield, CT: Millbrook Press, 2000.

Cole, Michael D. *Astronauts: Training for Space.* Berkeley Heights, NJ: Enslow Publishers, 1999.

Glenn, John, with Nick Taylor. *John Glenn: A Memoir.* New York: Bantam Books, 2000.

Green, Robert. *John Glenn: Astronaut and U.S. Senator.* New York: Ferguson Publishing, 2001.

Kramer, Barbara. *John Glenn: A Space Biography.* Berkeley Heights, NJ: Enslow Publishers, Inc., 1998.

Sipiera, Diane M., and Paul P. Sipiera. *Project Mercury.* Danbury, CT: Children's Press, 1997.

Vogt, Gregory L. *John Glenn's Return to Space.* Brookfield, CT: Millbrook Press, 2000.

Wolfe, Tom. *The Right Stuff.* New York: Bantam Doubleday Dell, 2001.

Zelon, Helen. *The Mercury 6 Mission: The 1st American Astronaut to Orbit Earth.* New York: The Rosen Publishing Group, Inc., 2002.

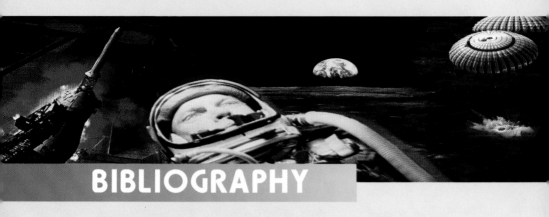

BIBLIOGRAPHY

Carpenter, Scott, and Kris Stoever. *For Spacious Skies: The Uncommon Journey of a Mercury Astronaut.* New York: Harcourt, 2003.

"*Chronology of John Herschel Glenn.*" The Ohio State University Archives, 1999. Retrieved May 2003 (http://www.lib.ohio-state.edu/arvweb/ glenn/glennchron.htm).

Collins, Michael. *Liftoff: The Story of America's Adventure in Space.* New York: Grove Press, 1988.

Glenn, John, with Nick Taylor. *John Glenn: A Memoir.* New York: Bantam Books, 2000.

Grant, R. G., and John R. Dailey. *Flight: 100 Years of Aviation.* New York: Dorling Kindersley Publishing, 2002.

"*John Glenn—Space Pioneer: Return to Orbit.*" NASA, 2000. Retrieved May 2003 (http://www. grc.nasa.gov/WWW/PAO/html/johnglen.htm).

Kraft, Chris. *Flight: My Life in Mission Control.* New York: E. P. Dutton, 2001.

Lethbridge, Cliff. *"History of Rocketry: Early 20th Century."* Spaceline.org, 2000. Retrieved May 2003 (http://www.spaceline.org/history/3.html).

Niccoli, Riccardo. *Book of Flight: From the Flying Machine of Leonardo Da Vinci to the Conquest of Space.* London: Sterling Publications, 2002.

Schirra, Wally. *Schirra's Space.* Annapolis, MD: United States Naval Institute Press, 1995.

Slayton, Donald K., et al. *Deke!: U.S. Manned Space: From Mercury to the Shuttle.* New York: Forge, 1995.

Swenson, Lloyd S., Jr., James M. Grimwod, and Charles C. Alexander. *This New Ocean: A History of Project Mercury.* Washington, DC: NASA Special Publications, 1989.

INDEX

About the Author

Paul Kupperberg is a freelance writer and an editor for DC Comics. He has published more than 700 comic books, stories, articles, and books, as well as several years' worth of the "Superman" and "Tom & Jerry" newspaper comic strips. Paul lives in Connecticut with his wife, Robin, and son, Max.

Photo Credits

Cover, pp. 1, 45, 47, 48, 52, 62, 64, 65, 67, 70, 81, 91, 93, 94 courtesy of NASA; pp. 4–5, 13, 26, 31, 35, 42, 73 (bottom), 74, 79, 82 © Bettmann/Corbis; p. 7 © Underwood and Underwood/Corbis; p. 8 © Baldwin H. Ward and Kathryn C. Ward/Corbis; p. 15 (left) courtesy of the John and Annie Glenn Historic Site; p. 15 (inset) © AP/Wide World Photos; p. 21 © classmates.com; p. 23 © Corbis; p. 37 courtesy of the U.S. Air Force Museum; p. 40 © Hulton/Getty/Archive/ Getty Images; p. 56 © Dean Conger/Corbis; p. 59 © NASA at Photori; p. 73 (top) © Time Life Pictures; p. 85 © Jacques M. Chenet/Corbis; p. 97 © AFP/Corbis.

Designer: Les Kanturek; Photo Researcher: Les Kanturek